Dahlia
Ravikovitch

A DRESS OF FIRE

Poems translated from the Hebrew
by
CHANA BLOCH

THE MENARD PRESS

A DRESS OF FIRE: poems in translation

Copyright © 1976 Chana Bloch

Preface to the poems
Copyright © 1976 Chana Bloch

Acknowledgments: See translator's note

Cover drawing by Tamara Rikman-Charny (Jerusalem)

We gratefully acknowledge the generous assistance of the Cultural and
Scientific Relations Division of Israel's Ministry of Foreign Affairs, given
through its Embassy in London.

ISBN 0 903400 28 6

The Menard Press is a member of the Association of Little Presses.

Menard Press books are exclusively distributed in the United States and
Canada by Serendipity Books Distribution, 1790 Shattuck Avenue,
Berkeley, California 94709, USA.

The Menard Press
23 Fitzwarren Gardens
London N19

Printed in Great Britain by Skelton's Press, Wellingborough, Northamptonshire.

CONTENTS

PREFACE

'Dahlia Ravikovitch writes as if she didn't have a skin,' a Jerusalem poet says of her work. What one is most aware of in reading her poems is the intense susceptibility to pain, her own and the world's. She writes about pain as if she were discovering a new truth: 'Pain has no use,/I assure you,' arguing with that adage which says there is always something to be made of pain. Desolation and loss is her subject: the aftershock of death, the deprivations of childhood, the brutality of adult relationships. Ravikovitch speaks with authority, with a piercing wisdom, about what happens 'when people break.' The note of disaster recurs almost obsessively, particularly in her personal poems: 'I nearly went under,' 'I fell on my face and shattered to bits,' 'I never thought I'd survive,' 'What's burning is me.'

'On the Road at Night . . . ,' from her first book, reveals perhaps the deepest source of her pain: her father was run over by a car when she was just six years old. In this tranced ballad-like poem, she tells how she returns to the scene of his death, searching him out, desperate to elicit from him 'one word of love.' It is a scene she must go on repeating forever: 'I will always have to,' she knows instinctively. She is possessed by the presence of the dead father whom she so loved and feared, whose death, one suspects, determines the course of the rest of her life.

'Only the Dust' evokes the misery of her childhood: she alone has no companion. Feeling the injustice keenly — how much she covets what all the world takes for granted! — she plots escapes to a magical happily-ever-after, promising herself 'I'd never come back, not as long as I lived.' In the very next line, though, she admits, 'But when I came back . . . . ' The moment she entertains the fantasy, she must concede defeat.

In 'Portrait,' the pathos that is just beneath the surface of so many of her poems gives way to a wry self-scrutiny.

5

Her demands are revealed as the caprice of a little girl who threatens to cry unless she has her way. In fact the insatiable child ('She wants vanilla') persists in the tough, disillusioned adult ('She wasn't born yesterday, if that's/what you're thinking'); the two voices, with various modifications of tone, are often heard together in Ravikovitch's poems.

The poet sees herself as badly used by those who cannot understand her. 'Clockwork Doll' recalls an experience of breakdown and partial recovery. Like Humpty Dumpty she has had a great fall, but as her luck would have it, 'they' — undefined and ominous — succeed in patching her together again. Yet she can never be as she was; fragile and tentative, she is shadowed by a sense of impending trouble. Wistfully she contemplates her own delicate beauty and blames the world which makes her its victim, subjecting her to the cruelty of its blundering expertise or calculated malice.

In 'The Dress' she is again the object of a kind of motiveless malignity. We are given no indication of why 'they made you/a dress of fire,' merely the terrible fact itself. As her friend grows increasingly frantic, trying to warn her, to save her, she can only reply with an abstracted helplessness, 'I don't know/how to be careful.' With a bold hand the poet brings together materials that are seemingly incompatible — an odd wisp of childhood memory and the high drama of Greek myth; 'the dress' refers of course to the poisoned wedding garment which Medea bestows on her rival Creusa.

Her love poems are about further varieties of pain. In 'Hills of Salt' she finds a powerful emblem for the loneliness of human relationships: the two immobilized figures who never touch, facing a sea where water, seaweed, light are all in voluptuous motion. 'The Noise of the Waters' follows the course of a destructive passion, violent as 'the ocean's pounding,' to the final convulsive loss of self. Most poignant perhaps is 'Time Caught in a Net,' with its impossible reverie of 'so much love.'

Ravikovitch does not write about the trauma of the concentration camps or of Israel's wars, subjects which preoccupy other contemporary Israeli poets. The world she creates is often exotic in its trappings: one thinks of the European emigrés in Chad and Cameroon who are 'sick of life,' the crusaders who 'plundered everything,' the citizens of Hong Kong who, even on doomsday, go on mauling the 'little prostitutes.' Her Hong Kong is a compelling symbol for the sensual splendour and degradation of the modern world. Ravikovitch succeeds in rendering the vulgar extravagance of the *dolce vita* along with its mindless barbarity. A solitary witness to the fate of Hong Kong ('I alone knew'), she contemplates its destruction with an apocalyptic fury.

If her subjects are exotic, her diction, at any rate, is traditional in the way it assimilates the language of Bible and Midrash. Some of her early poems, indeed, are almost a mosaic of biblical and midrashic allusions, to the despair of a translator; in this selection, I have deliberately omitted the most allusive of her poems. Even her recent work, looser in form and more colloquial in tone, incorporates such references without the slightest incongruity.

The habit of biblical allusion may seem studied or 'literary' to a reader of contemporary English poetry, but it is perfectly commonplace in Hebrew. In finding titles for her books, for example, Ravikovitch quite naturally turns to the Bible. For her volume of selected verse, *All Thy Breakers and Waves,* she takes a phrase from Psalm 42.7 (translation from New English Bible):
    Deep calls to deep in the roar of thy cataracts,
    and all thy waves, all thy breakers, pass over me.

And the title of her latest book — literally *Deep Calls* — abbreviates the opening words of the very same verse. The fact that she can employ this ellipsis suggests the familiarity with the Bible which can be expected of the reader of Hebrew. In English this kind of biblical shorthand is nearly impossible; if one does not point up the allusion in some fashion, it is in danger of going unrecognized. Searching for a way to translate this title — *Deep*

Calls, The Deep Calls, The Call of the Deep! — I finally settled on the formal quotation in its archaic King James form — *Deep Calleth Unto Deep* — as a way of preserving the allusion. There would have been some logic in choosing one of Ravikovitch's psalm titles for the present collection, but it should now be clear to the reader why I decided not to do so.

The apocalyptic fervour of 'How Hong Kong was Destroyed' takes a different turn in 'The Blue West.' Here Ravikovitch is a prophet of glad tidings, a voice in the wilderness crying out that the crooked shall be made straight. She stands in the bleakness of no-man's land with its stones, its ruins, dreaming of 'the other side of the hill.' Repeating 'I want . . . I want . . . If only' like an incantation, she conjures up is a vision of redemption: 'On one of the days to come/ . . . a sun will shine for us.' But like the 'infinite treasures' she needs to believe in, it is hopelessly out of reach.

After the high pitch of her yearning there is, in the recent poems, written in her late thirties, a sense of resignation, of accommodation, of minimal expectations. She is sailing off nowhere — not to the land of Cathay, Madagascar, the isles of the sun, the blue west. She sits solitary in her room, in a world where day and night are 'equally silent' and 'nothing's waiting for me.' It is a world of radically reduced circumstances. She is alone with herself, with her poems, with the birds outside her window. The image of the bird's feather which falls unnoticed focuses precisely her sense of drift and abandonment. The birds, at least, are not 'malicious'. In their flight she sees an intimation of ease, of grace; in their song she manages to hear 'a note of compassion,' perhaps the only redemption we can hope to know.

CHANA BLOCH

TRANSLATOR'S NOTE

The poems in this volume represent a selection from Dahlia Ravikovitch's work from 1959 to the present. They are not in chronological order. Some of the translations have appeared, or will appear shortly, in *The American Poetry Review, Café Solo, Hyperion, Modern Poetry in Translation, Shantih* and *Tri-quarterly,* as well as in *Fourteen Israeli Poets* (André Deutsch), *The Other Voice* (W. W. Norton), *New Writing from Israel* (Corgi) and the forthcoming *Penguin Anthology of Women Poets.*

I would like to thank Diana O Hehir, Stephen Mitchell, Robert Friend, Del Marie Rogers, Dennis Silk, Anita Barrows and Carol Cosman for their helpful criticism: my husband Ariel Bloch, for his generous collaboration; and finally, Dahlia Ravikovitch, with whom it has been a great pleasure to work.

C.B.

9

If there was just a road there
the ruins of workshops
one fallen minaret
and some carcasses of machines,
why couldn't I
come to the heart of the field?
There is nothing more painful
than a field
with a stone on its heart.

I want to reach the other side of the hill,
want to reach
want to be there.
I want to break out of the mass of the earth,
from my head to my footsoles
the mass of the earth.

I want to reach the ends of thought
whose beginnings
slice like a knife.
I want to climb up to the fringes of the sun
and not be eaten by fire.

If only we could walk about
with grasshopper feet on the water,
If only we could climb
a great arch of the sun's rays,

If only we could reach
all the cities beyond the sea —
And here is another sorrow:
a seashore where there are no ships.

On one of the days to come
the eye of the sea will darken
with the multitude of ships.
In that hour all the mass of the earth
will be spread as a cloth.

And a sun will shine for us blue as the sea,
a sun will shine for us warm as an eye,
will wait until we climb up
as it heads for the blue west.

On the road at night there stands the man
Who once upon a time was my father.
And I must come to the place where he stands
Because I was his eldest daughter.

And night after night he stands there alone in his place
And I must go down to his place and be there.
And I want to ask the man how long will I have to.
And I know, even as I ask, I will always have to.

In the place where he stands there is a fear of danger
Like the day he was walking along and a car ran him over.
And that's how I knew him and I found ways to remember
That this was the man who once was my father.

And he doesn't tell me one word of love
Though once upon a time he was my father.
And even though I was his eldest daughter
He cannot tell me one word of love.

Then that stranger walked away
a shred of ivy clung to his shoes
his scarf knotted around his neck
and the wind gored him

The larks were whistling
starlings hung in the clouds
and the skies were filled with the ravens' shrieking
the terror of sunset, the glare
of the rose

And a wisp of straw that lifted in the wind
flashed and glinted like one of the stars

Light and shade were clusters of grapes
black and green, dangling
from a twig

And a wisp of straw that lifted in the wind
fluttered and fell between the ravens' wings

And then that stranger walked away
a shred of ivy clung to his shoes
his scarf knotted around his neck
and the wind
gored him

REQUIEM

The cantor was reading Psalms.
The trees whispered
like a flock of black priests.

We were not much taller than the gravestones
and we knew there would be
no resurrection in our day.

The ladder reached up from there
to the ranks of the holy and pure
who shine like sapphire
(most of them lay at our feet).

Our lives were like a grasshopper's
on the border of sun and shade.

But when the drowned girl passed through
all the chambers of the sea
we knew

it is the sea
that gives life to the rivers.

MEMORY

Only when the face is blotted out
can you remember anything fully,
only when the face
vanishes.

First the lights go wild,
the colors start from their frames.
Stars plunge from their heights like epileptics.
Grasses moan,
the new growth more painful
than wilting.

Whatever plasters our eyes
retreats to the shadows.
And the face, too.
Something stirs in the depths.

How many days, years,
thunderstorms
have we waited
for one innocent memory
to break from the depths of the earth
clear red as a poppy.

Think of it: only the dust
followed me,
I had no other companion.
Trailed me to the kindergarten,
tangled my hair
on the warmest days.

Just think who was at my side
and all my friends had another.
When winter spread terrible slings in the sky,
when the clouds gulped their prey,
imagine who kept me company
and how much
I wanted another.

The pine cones rustled, and for a while
I ached to be alone with the wind.
Nights I dreamed in a fever
about houses drenched
with love.
Imagine how I was cheated if the dust
was my only companion.

On the days of the hot wind, I'd sail
for the city of the leviathans,
full of a wild happiness.
I'd never come back, not as long as I lived.

But when I came back,
I was like a raven
whose cousins the ravens hated her.
I had no companion at all, and only
the dust
kept me company.

Tonight I came back in a sailing boat
From the isles of the sun and the coral reefs.
Maidens with golden combs in their hair
Stayed onshore in the isles of the sun.

Four years of honey and milk
I wandered onshore in the isles of the sun.
The fruit stands were always laden,
The cherries flashed in the sun.

Sailors and boatswains from seventy lands
Sailed for the isles of the sun.
Four years in that streaming light
I would count the golden ships.

Four years round as an apple
I braided chaplets of coral.
Merchants and peddlers in the isles of the sun
Spread their lengths of crimson silk.

And the sea was deeper than deep
When I came back from the isles of the sun.
Drops of sun heavy as honey
Fell on the island when the sun went down.

CLOCKWORK DOLL

That night, I was a clockwork doll,
And I turned round and round, to the left and the right,
And I fell on my face and shattered to bits,
And they tried to patch me with all of their skill.

And once again, I was a proper doll,
My manner carefully poised and polite.
But I'd become a doll of a different sort,
A broken twig that only a tendril holds.

And then I went out to dance at the ball,
But they left me with a rabble of dogs and cats
Though all my steps were measured and rhythmical.

And I had blue eyes and I had golden hair
And I had a dress the color of garden flowers
And I had a trimming of cherries on my straw hat.

And again I was like one of those little girls,
my nails black with work,
building tunnels in the sand.

Wherever my eye stopped
there were bands of purple
and many eyes shining like silver pearls.

Again I was like one of those little girls
who sail in one night around the whole world
and sail to the land of Cathay
and Madagascar,

and who smash plates and saucers
from so much love,
so much love,
so much love.

Foam fluttered on the sea like birds' wings.
Two salt hills were left on the beach,
and the sea was a welter of pools,
with sailboats small as a finger
gleaming
like soap bubbles.

The two of us sat, each by his pool,
two sand strips between us
and a wealth of seaweed.
The heavy fronds swayed back and forth,
grasping at the teeth of the rocks in their lust.

A mass of seaweed broke loose and fell at my feet,
and my eyelids were heavy with sun.
And the sea rose up and spilled over
from pool to pool,
blue streams in a net of light.

Pools lapped at the palms of our hands,
the sand between us — the length of two arms.
We did not draw near all that day,
not by a hairsbreadth,
our bodies two salt hills and our feet seaweed.

A bird twittered like crazy
till it could no more
and then it wept

I sank in a cloud of pleasure
I sank
oh I melted away.

But no I was drowned in the ocean
there a man loved me
didn't leave me a fingernail.

His hand caught me by the hair
in the ocean's pounding
I nearly went under.

His hand
dragged me by the hair
in the teeming ocean

I no longer
remember
a thing.

PRIDE

Even rocks crack, I tell you,
and not because of age.
For years they lie on their backs
in the heat and the cold,
so many years,
it almost seems peaceful.
They don't move, so the cracks stay hidden.
A kind of pride.
Years pass over them, waiting.
Whoever is going to shatter them
hasn't come yet.
And so the moss flourishes, the seaweed swirls,
the sea pushes through and rolls back,
and it seems they are motionless.
Till a little seal comes to rub against the rocks,
comes and goes away.
And suddenly the stone is split.
I told you, when people break it happens by surprise.

In the morning strange ships appeared on the sea,
prow and stern
in the ancient fashion.
In eleven hundred, bands of crusaders set sail,
kings and rabble.
Crates of gold and plunder piled up in the ports,
ships of gold
piers of gold.
The sun lit marvelous flames in them,
burning forests.
When the sun dazzled and the waves rocked,
they longed for Byzantium.
How cruel and simple the crusaders were.
They plundered everything.

Terror seized the villagers.
Those strangers carried off their daughters,
sired them blue-eyed grandsons
in shame,
shrugged off their honor.

Slender-necked ships set sail for Egypt.
The splendid troops struck at Acre,
a lightning force.
All of them swift knights bearing the Bishop's blessing.
A great flock of wolves.
How their eyes shone
when they saw the palm trees sway in the wind.
How they soiled their beards with spittle
when they dragged women into the brush.
They built many citadels,
snipers' towers and ramparts of basalt.
Their bastards in the villages
marvelled at them.

In twelve hundred, the Marquis of Montfort
grew faint.
The winds of Galilee whistled over his gloomy fortress.
A curved dagger burst from the East —
a jester's staff.
Saladin, in motley, advanced from the East.
With a ram's horns that infidel
gored them hip upon thigh,
punished them
at the Horns of Hittin.

No kingdom remained to them,
no life eternal,
no Jerusalem.
How cruel and simple the crusaders were.
They plundered everything.

IN CHAD AND CAMEROON

By the waters of Chad and Cameroon
Europeans live who are sick of life.
They no longer care about manners.

Not far from them
a band of lepers passes by.
Old men without fingers.

When evening comes, the wind
doesn't stir.
It is hot, as in the beginning.

Only a pink glow rises from the waters
in Chad and Cameroon
and falls on the Europeans.

I am in Hong Kong.
There's a river here swarming with snakes.
There are Greeks, Chinese, Negroes.
Carnival dragons
gape at the paper lanterns.
Who said they eat you alive here?
A great crowd went down to the river.
You've never seen such silk in your life,
redder than poppy blossoms.

In Hong Kong
the sun rises in the East
and they water the flowers with a perfumed spray
to double their scent.
But the evening wind batters the paper lanterns,
and if someone's murdered, they ask,
Was it a Chinaman? a Negro?
Did he die in pain?
Then they pitch his body into the river
and all the reptiles feed.

I am in Hong Kong.
In the evening the café lights dimmed
and paper lanterns ripped in the streets.
The ground seethed and exploded
seethed and exploded
and I alone knew
there is nothing in the West
and nothing in the East.

The paper dragon yawned
but the ground exploded.
Enemies will come here
who've never seen silk in their lives.

Only the little prostitutes
dressed in soiled silk
still receive their guests

in tiny alcoves crowded with lanterns.
In the morning they
cry over their rotting flesh.
And if someone's killed, they ask,
Chinaman, Negro? Poor thing.
Let's hope he didn't die painfully.
And at dusk the first
of the visitors arrive
like a thorn in the living flesh.

I am in Hong Kong
and Hong Kong hangs on the ocean
like a colored lantern on a hook
at the end of the world.
Perhaps the dragon
will swathe it in crimson silk
and let it drop
into the abyss of the stars.
And only the little prostitutes will sob into the silk
because even now
still now
men pinch them in the belly.

I am not in Hong Kong
and Hong Kong is not in the world.
Where Hong Kong used to be
there's a reddish stain
half in the water and half in the sky.

A PERSONAL OPINION

Pain has no use,
I assure you:
a worm in a piece of fruit
won't make the fruit taste better.
I know you,
I can see what your youth did to you,
how your face grows haggard.
That's not the way heroes are made.

Heroes are different, it seems to me,
they don't grow like potatoes.
They fight in the air, on sea,
even in Manchuria.
How my heart goes out to them in the air, on sea —
but let them not dream of medals.
As a rule they're used for stoking up locomotives
as in Manchuria,
and I'm sorry to say they die like dogs.

Pain is inhuman,
I insist,
there are no extenuating circumstances.
Look, isn't it monstrous:
someone secretly dying away,
growing blacker and blacker,
withering,
without a wife, without sons.

THE DRESS

for Yitzhak Livni

You know, she said, they made you
a dress of fire.
Remember how Jason's wife burned in her dress?
It was Medea, she said, Medea did that to her.
You've got to be careful, she said.
They made you a dress that glows
like an ember, that burns like coals.

Do you want to wear it, she said, don't wear it.
It's not the wind whistling,
it's the poison spreading.
You're not a princess, what can you do to Medea?
You must tell one sound from another, she said,
it's not the wind whistling.

Remember, I told her, that time when I was six?
They shampooed my hair and I went outside like that.
The smell of shampoo trailed after me like a cloud.
Afterwards I was sick from the wind and the rain.
I didn't know yet how to read Greek tragedies
but the smell of the perfume spread
and I was very sick.
Now I realize it's an unnatural perfume.

What will become of you, she said,
they made you a burning dress.
They made me a burning dress, I said, I know it.
So why are you standing there, she said,
you've got to be careful,
don't you know what a burning dress is?

I know, I said, but I don't know
how to be careful.
The smell of that perfume confuses me.
I said to her, No one has to agree with me,
I have no faith in Greek tragedies.

But the dress, she said, the dress is on fire.
What are you saying, I shouted,
what are you saying?
I'm not wearing a dress at all,
what's burning is me.

HARD WINTER

The little mulberry shook in the flame
and before its glory vanished
it was lapped in sadness.

Rain and sun ruled by turns, and in the house
we were afraid to think
what would become of us.

The plants reddened at their hearts
and the pool lay low.
Each of us was sunk in himself alone.

But for an instant, off-guard,
I saw
how men topple from this world

like a tree that lightning splits
heavy with limbs and flesh, the wet branches
trampled like dead grass.

The shutter was worn and the walls thin.
Rain and sun, by turns, rode over us
with iron wheels.

All the fibres of the plants were intent
on themselves alone.
This time I never thought I'd survive.

TWO SONGS OF THE GARDEN

1

Some ants found half a dead fly
and they had a hard time
dragging it off the grass.
Their tiny backs cracked with the strain.
Just then the grass bristled
all at once, like a barley field.
What madness, that the grass
should think itself a barley field.
I knew the ants' fate would be bitter:
all that hard labor, and an early death.
A few well-fed insects poked about in the grass
and the silly ants had to hear their droning.
Every one of the flowers bloomed
as well as it could,
the roses more showy than last year.
Then I had to cry.
Beside me
all of them had become
such giants.

2

A swarm of gnats seethes every day at six.
My poor grass grows hunchback.
Every day I want to ask for something.
The sun no longer seems like a ball of fire,
it's seething within.
No air to breathe, there is only
pleading.
I tell you, if this summer passes,
everything will return
where it belongs.
The flower to the plant, the bird's wing.
The sand that wandered off will make its way back
to the bay.
With a few stalks of corn and some leaves

stricken by aphids
it's impossible to live.
I tell you it's impossible to live.

So many things sprouting
and almost none of them
in bloom.

PORTRAIT

She sits in the house for days on end.
She reads the papers.
(What's the matter, don't you?)
She doesn't do what she'd like to do,
things get in the way.
She wants vanilla, lots of vanilla,
give her vanilla.

In winter she's cold, really cold,
colder than other people.
She bundles up but she's still cold.
She wants vanilla.

She wasn't born yesterday, if that's
what you're thinking.
This isn't the first time she's felt the cold.
Not the first time it's winter.
In fact summer isn't so pleasant either.
She reads the papers more than she'd like to.
In winter she won't budge without the heater.
Sometimes she gets fed up.
Did she ever ask you for much?
You'll admit she hasn't.
She wants vanilla.

If you'll look closely, she's
got a tartan skirt.
She likes a tartan skirt because it's sporty.
Just to look at her, you'd laugh.
Even she laughs about it sometimes.
She has a hard time in winter,
a rough time in summer,
you'd laugh.

Call her mimosa,
a bird without wings,
call her whatever you like.
She's always wrapping herself up in something

and stifling,
sometimes a tartan skirt and other stuff.
Why wrap herself up if it's stifling?
These things are complicated.
It's the cold in winter, the impossible
heat in summer,
never the way you want it.

And by the way, don't forget,
she wants vanilla.
Now she's even crying.
Give her vanilla.

TRYING

Remember you promised to come
on the holiday
an hour after dark.
I've left debts in a number of places,
would you care to settle them?
Since you'll be coming after dark
no one will be watching you.
Since you'll be coming after dark
I'll be watching you.

It's hard to understand why the house,
though it's heated, doesn't get warm.
It seems to me that the walls
are writhing with pain
inside the plaster.
Yet we ourselves push it all away
from day to day, to the end of days.
Look, it's a fraud
that we should act as if we
were the sons of the gods.

Remember you promised to come
on the holiday
an hour after dark.
For my part, I won't be keeping
a tally of grudges
till you come.
And you — don't believe what I say
when it's perverse or marvellous.
I go to sleep like everyone else
and I don't practice magic.
I forgo the honors in advance.
I'm no daughter of the gods.
Remember when and where.

To be a marionette.
In this gray, precious light before dawn
to drift under the new day
pulled
by the undercurrents.
To be a marionette,
a pale fragile china doll
held by threads.

To be a marionette.
The threads on which my whole life depends
are real silk.
A marionette,
she too is real.
She has memories.

Four hundred years ago
she was Doña Elvira, Countess of Seville,
with three hundred chambermaids.
And only when she glanced at
her fine silk handkerchief
did she know her fate:
she would be a china marionette
or a wax doll.

Doña Elvira, Countess of Seville,
dreamt of late-ripening vines.
Her knights always spoke softly to her.
Doña Elvira, the Countess and so forth,
was gathered unto her people.
She left two sons and a daughter
to a gloomy future.

In the twentieth century, in a gray, precious dawn,
how fortunate
to be a marionette.
This woman is not responsible for her actions,
say the judges.
Her fragile heart is gray as the dawn.
Her body is held by threads.

EVEN A THOUSAND YEARS

I can't remake the world
and there's no sense in it either.
Day unto day and day unto night declare nothing.
In the spring, sweet-pea, lilacs and roses come up,
everything life-size and in natural color.
Nothing really new grows here,
not once in ten years.

Whoever wants attar of roses,
let him gather it from the wind,
and whoever wants to plant, let him plant a fig-tree
for the generations to come.

You ask if I've ever seen beauty?
Well, I've seen quite a bit,
but not in the right places.
Say, a waterfall:
of course I've seen it, so what?
It's not a pleasant sight.
Beauty doesn't walk about in the street,
sometimes it's inside a room
when the doors are locked and the shutters down.
I know too much about such things to fool myself
and settle for less.

After the pain there's just curiosity
to see what happens in the end
to everything beautiful.

Of course I don't have to plant a fig-tree:
there are other ways.
I can wait for spring, the roses, the hyacinths.

But in time people grow tough
as fingernails,
gray, stubborn as stone.
One is tempted to become a block of salt
with a mineral strength.
To gaze
empty-eyed at this potash and phosphate factory
even a thousand years.

SURELY YOU REMEMBER

After they all leave,
I remain alone with the poems,
some poems of mine, some of others.
I prefer poems by others.
I remain quiet, and the choking stops.
I remain.

Sometimes I wish everyone would go away.
Perhaps it's nice to write poems.
You sit in your room and the walls grow taller.
Colors deepen.
A blue kerchief becomes the depth of a well.

You wish everyone would go away.
You don't know what's bothering you.
Perhaps you'll think of something.
Then it all passes and you are pure crystal.

After that, love.
Narcissus was so much in love with himself.
Only a fool doesn't understand
he loved the river, too.

You sit alone.
Your heart grieves you, but it won't break.
The faded images wash away one by one.
Then the blemishes.
A sun sets at midnight. You remember
the dark flowers, too.

You wish you were dead or alive or
somebody else.
Perhaps there's a single country you love?
a single word?
Surely you remember.

Only a fool lets the sun set when it likes.
It always drifts off too early
westward to the islands.

Sun and moon, winter and summer
will come to you,
infinite treasures.

FROM DAY TO NIGHT

Every day I wake up again
as if for the last time.
I don't know what's waiting for me,
perhaps that's a sign
that nothing's waiting for me.

This spring
is like the spring before.
I know what the month of Iyyar means,
but it means nothing to me.
I can't tell the moment
that divides day from night,
just that night is colder
though both are equally silent.

At dawn I hear the sound of birds
and my affection for them
eases me to sleep.
The one I care for isn't here,
perhaps he is nowhere.

I go from day to day
from day to night
like a feather
the bird doesn't feel
as it falls.

This chirping
is not in the least malicious.
They sing without giving us a thought
and they are as many
as the seed of Abraham.
They have a life of their own.
Flight comes naturally to them.
Some are rare, some common,
but the wing itself is grace.
Their hearts are not heavy
even when they peck at a worm.
Perhaps they're light-headed.
The heavens were given to them
to rule over day and night
and when they alight on a branch,
the branch is theirs too.
Their chirping is entirely free
of malice. Over the years
it seems
one even hears in it
a note of compassion.

Dahlia Ravikovitch, one of Israel's leading poets, was born in Tel Aviv in 1936. Educated at the Hebrew University in Jerusalem, she has worked as a journalist and teacher. Her first book of poetry, *The Love of an Orange* (1959), immediately established her reputation. It was followed by *A Hard Winter* (1964) and *The Third Book* (1969); a selection from these volumes, *All Thy Breakers and Waves* (1972); and most recently, *Deep Calleth Unto Deep* (1976). In addition she has published a volume of short stories and essays, *A Death in the Family* (1976). This collection of poetry introduces her work to the English-reading public.

Chana Faerstein Bloch was born in New York City in 1940. She studied at Cornell, Brandeis, and the University of California at Berkeley, where she received her Ph.D. in 1975 with a dissertation on 'George Herbert and the Bible.' She now lives in Berkeley and teaches English Literature at Mills College. Her poems, as well as her translations from Yiddish and Hebrew, have been published widely. In 1974 she was a winner of the Discovery Award of the YM-YWHA Poetry Center in New York.